Quick Tricks for Story Time

by Annalisa McMorrow
illustrated by Marilynn G. Barr

This book is dedicated to
Devon.

Publisher: Roberta Suid
Design & Production: Little Acorn & Associates, Inc.

Entire contents copyright © 2002 by
Monday Morning Books, Inc.
For a complete catalog, please write to the address below:

P.O. Box 1134
Inverness, CA 94937

E-mail us at: MMBooks@aol.com
Visit our Web site: www.mondaymorningbooks.com
Call us at: 1-800-255-6049

ISBN 1-57612-161-5

Printed in the United States of America
987654321

Contents

Introduction 4
Goldilocks and the Three Bears 6
The Very Busy Spider 8
Green Eggs and Ham 10
Goodnight Moon 12
Bunny Money 14
Five Little Monkeys 16
Corduroy 18
Good Night, Gorilla 20
The Mitten 22
Ten Apples Up On Top! 24
Blue Hat, Green Hat 26
Mr. Brown Can Moo! Can You? 28
Sheep In a Jeep 30
Mouse Paint 32
Chrysanthemum 34
A Color of His Own 36
Harold and the Purple Crayon 38
Blueberries for Sal 40
I Went Walking 42
The Shape of Me 44
The Jolly Postman 46
Pat the Bunny 48
The Wheels on the Bus 50
Miss Mary Mack 52
I'm a Little Teapot 54
Make Way for Ducklings 56
Mr. Rabbit and the Lovely Present 58
Where the Wild Things Are 60
It Looked Like Spilt Milk 62
If You Give a Moose a Muffin 64
The Carrot Seed 66
The Three Little Pigs 68

The Stupids Step Out 70
Curious George Gets a Medal 72
Strega Nona 74
Mushroom in the Rain 76
Madeline 78
The Rainbow Fish 80
Caps for Sale 82
Little Red Riding Hood 84
Cloudy with a Chance of Meatballs 86
The Lady with the Alligator Purse 88
Bugs in a Box 90
One Fine Day 92
Clifford, the Big Red Dog 94
Tikki Tikki Tembo 96

Introduction

Storybooks open new worlds for young children. They become engaged in the colorful pictures as well as the words. Once a child has heard a book several times, he or she will often be able to "read" along with you.

The activities in *Quick Tricks for Story Time* draw inspiration from favorite children's books, extending the enjoyment by adding an activity to story time. All that is required to make storybooks come to life are the provided patterns and everyday props such as a bowl or a spool of thread. Engaging the children in an activity will reinforce the story. Children will soon be retelling the stories to you, to each other, and to families and friends.

Often storybooks provide more than a few minutes of diversion. If you pay careful attention, there are many teaching opportunities presented by famous children's books. For instance, *The Very Hungry Caterpillar* teaches the days of the week (as well as providing an excellent opening for a discussion of the values of proper nutrition). *Alexander and the Terrible, Horrible, No Good, Very Bad Day* provides an opportunity to explore different feelings, as well as the fact that everyone has a bad day sometimes. You'll find counting tie-ins in stories such as *The Three Little Pigs*, and information about animals can be found in *Is Your Mama a Llama?* and in *The Very Busy Spider*.

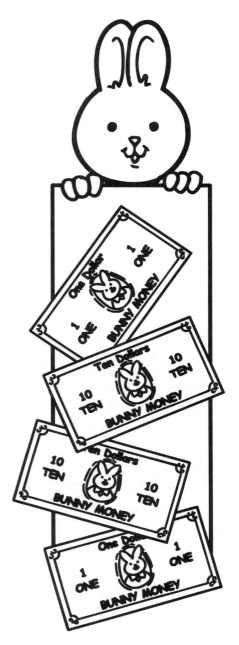

Because teachers work on tight schedules, the activities in *Quick Tricks for Story Time* are just that: quick! Most have fewer than six materials listed and can be done in a matter of minutes. Set-up and clean-up are minimal. However, most of the activities may easily be extended by reading a suggested book link or doing one of the options listed at the bottom of each project.

Included for each activity is a page of multi-purpose patterns. These whimsical drawings can be duplicated onto heavy paper for use as puppets, enlarged and colored for classroom bulletin board decorations, or easily transformed into desk or cubby labels. Consider copying this page and sending it home with children to share with their families. Children can color the drawings or draw their own after looking at the ones provided.

Gather a variety of your favorite storybooks for storage in your reading corner. Children can view the pictures in these books during free time, recognizing the tales that you have already read to them.

Be on the lookout for other ways to extend your story time. Some storybooks now have game board tie-ins, such as *Miss Spider's Tea Party* and *Stellaluna*. Others are available on cassette or CD for the children's personal listening pleasure. Still more have been featured on puzzles. Use these types of products to reinforce the stories that you choose to share with the children.

Some of the stories in this book are by a specific author, such as *Bunny Money* by Rosemary Wells. Others, such as *Goldilocks and the Three Bears*, have been illustrated many times by different artists. Choose your favorite of these versions to read. You'll find that most of the books can be found in board book editions.

Goldilocks and the Three Bears
A Quick Trick with Bowls

Learning about sizes is fun when the activity is linked to a famous story.

Materials:
Three plastic bowls of different sizes

Directions:
1. Gather the children in a circle.
2. Read or tell the story of Goldilocks and the Three Bears. When you get to the part about the porridge, place the bowls in the middle of the circle. Have the children help you set the bowls from biggest (for Papa Bear) to smallest (for Baby Bear).
3. Store the bowls and a book about Goldilocks in a place where children can act out the story on their own.

Options:
• Add additional props to the story. For instance, you might bring in three different-sized chairs.
• This story can be used as a lead-in for snack time. Serve porridge (or oatmeal).
• Use the patterns on the next page to make puppets for use with the telling of this story. Duplicate the patterns onto heavy paper. Cut out the patterns, and add craft stick handles.

Book Link:
The Three Bears by Byron Barton

Goldilocks and the Three Bears

The Very Busy Spider
A Quick Trick with Yarn

Children will create a cooperative classroom spider web while you read this engaging story. Discuss how some spiders spin webs to catch their meals.

Materials:
Yarn

Directions:
1. Tie the free end of a ball of yarn to an object, such as a table.
2. Gather the children in a circle and give one child the ball of yarn. That child is the spider.
3. Start to read *The Very Busy Spider*. When you reach the refrain ("but the spider was very busy") have the child wrap the yarn around another object and then hand the ball to the next child.
4. Continue reading the story and having the children create a yarn web in the classroom. Make sure that every child has a chance to string the yarn web to an object.
5. At the end of the story, the children can work together to unravel the web.

Options:
• Have different children act out the parts of the animals on the farm who approach the spider.
• Use the patterns on the next page to make puppets for use with the telling of this story. Duplicate the patterns onto heavy paper. Cut out the patterns, and add craft stick handles.

Book Link:
The Very Busy Spider by Eric Carle

Green Eggs and Ham
A Quick Trick with Green Chalk

This activity provides an opportunity to discuss color words, trying new foods, and eating properly.

Materials:
Green chalk (or green crayons)
White paper

Directions:
1. Read the story to the children.
2. Give each child a sheet of white paper and a piece of green chalk or a green crayon.
3. Have the children draw their own versions of green food. They do not need to draw green eggs and ham. They might draw green spaghetti or green bananas.
4. Let the children talk about their drawings. Then post the completed drawings on a "Green Food" bulletin board.

Options:
• Serve green foods at snack time. You might have the children try celery, broccoli, zucchini, green apples, and green beans.
• Use the patterns on the next page for children to use in their art project. Duplicate the patterns onto heavy paper. Cut out the patterns, and add craft stick handles.

Book Link:
Green Eggs and Ham by Dr. Seuss

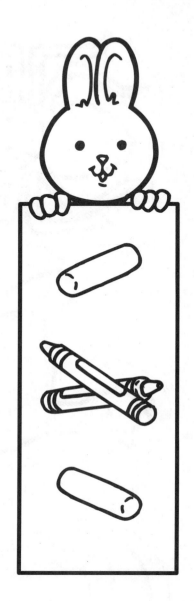

Goodnight Moon
A Quick Trick with a Clock

This activity is one way to introduce time-telling skills.

Materials:
Clock

Directions:
1. Set the clock to seven.
2. Gather the children around the clock and read them the story. The time progresses in the story, so change the hands on the clock as you turn the pages.
3. Read the story several times. Pause and let the children help you read the clock each time you reset it.

Options:
• Gather assorted props that are featured in the story, such as a comb and a brush, mittens, socks, a telephone, and a stuffed mouse. As you read the story, the children can take turns holding up the props.
• Use the patterns on the next page to make puppets for use with the telling of this story. Duplicate the patterns onto heavy paper. Cut out the patterns, and add craft stick handles.

Book Link:
Goodnight Moon by Margaret Wise Brown

Goodnight Moon

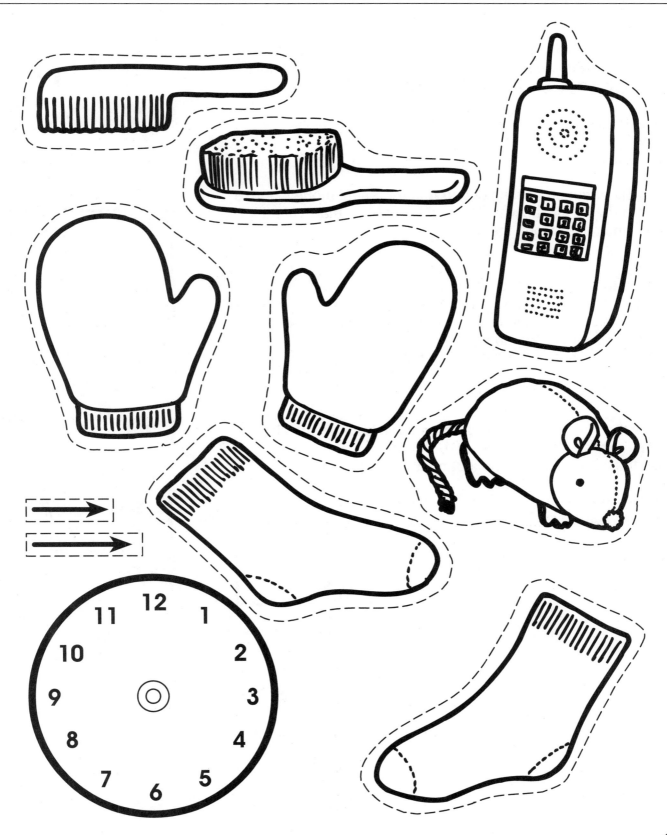

Bunny Money
A Quick Trick with a Wallet

Max learns about the value of money when he and Ruby go to buy their grandmother a birthday present. Children will enjoy counting the money that Max and Ruby spend.

Materials:
Wallet
Paper money

Note: Either cut out pieces of paper to represent money, or use play money for this activity. The wallet could be made of paper, folded and taped along the sides.

Directions:
1. Place the money in the wallet.
2. Gather the children around and read the story.
3. When Max and Ruby spend money, have a child take out the correct amount of play money.
4. Give each child an opportunity to remove money from the wallet.

Options:
• Store the play money and wallet near the book where children can act out the story on their own.
• Use the patterns on the next page to make play money.

Book Link:
Bunny Money by Rosemary Wells

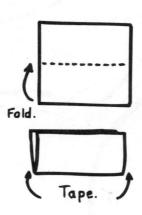

Fold.

Tape.

Place money in wallet.

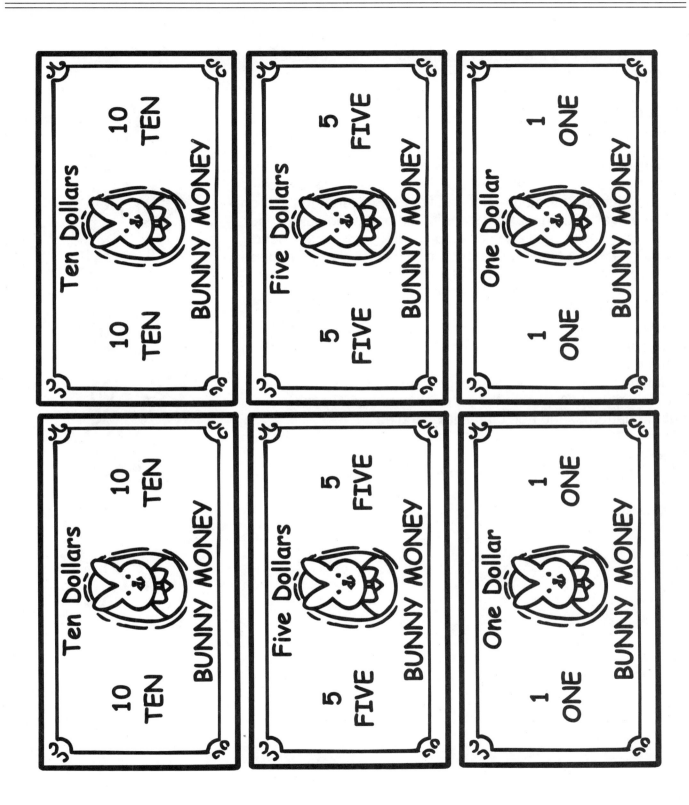

Five Little Monkeys
A Quick Trick with a Mat

This book provides the perfect subtraction activity. Let the children join in as you read the story.

Materials:
Mats

Directions:
1. Do this activity in an area where the children have a lot of space to jump. Spread mats on the floor for children to jump on.
2. Have five children start by standing up and jumping. As you tell the story, one child should sit down with each verse. Read the story enough times for each child to have a chance to be a monkey. (The children who are sitting should help count how many monkeys remain upright after each verse.)

Options:
• Start with a higher number of monkeys, such as ten, and then count down.
• Use the patterns on the next page to make puppets for use with this rhyme. Duplicate the patterns onto heavy paper. Cut out the patterns, and add craft stick handles.

Book Link:
Five Little Monkeys Jumping on the Bed by Eileen Christelow

Five Little Monkeys

Corduroy
A Quick Trick with Lids

A bear missing a button provides a perfect opportunity for a counting activity.

Materials:
Plastic lids
Permanent marker

Directions:
1. Draw button holes on the lids using the marker.
2. Read the story of *Corduroy* to the children. In the story, Corduroy is missing a button.
3. Set the "button" lids on the floor for the children to count. Use as many lids as would be appropriate for your children's level of counting skills.

Option:
Use the patterns on the next page to make bears and buttons. Duplicate the patterns onto heavy paper. Color code for a color-matching activity, or program with numerals and dots for a number-matching activity. (The numerals would go on the bears and the dots would be "holes" on the buttons.)

Book Link:
Corduroy by Don Freeman

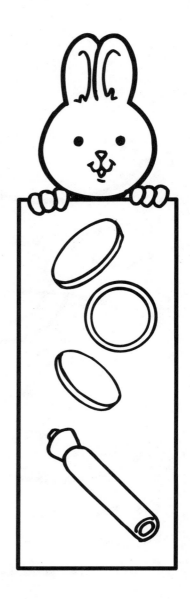

Good Night, Gorilla
A Quick Trick with Keys

Most children have a fascination with keys. This activity ties in to a feature of the delightful story.

Materials:
Colored plastic keys
Shoe boxes
Colored construction paper
Glue

Directions:
1. Create a color-matching game by covering shoe boxes with different colored construction paper. Make a box for each colored key that you have.
2. Read the story *Good Night, Gorilla* to the children. In it, the gorilla uses a different colored key to unlock different cages and set the animals free. Each key matches the color on each cage.
3. Have the children match the colored keys to the colored shoe box "cages."

Options:
• Place different plastic animals in the shoe box "cages" for the children to set free.
• Use colored key protectors on real keys.
• Use the patterns on the next page to make a set of keys for each child. Duplicate the keys onto heavy paper and cut out. Punch a hole in each. String together on a piece of yarn for a key ring. Have the children color each key using the correct color of crayon or marker.

Book Link:
Good Night, Gorilla by Peggy Rathmann

Good Night, Gorilla

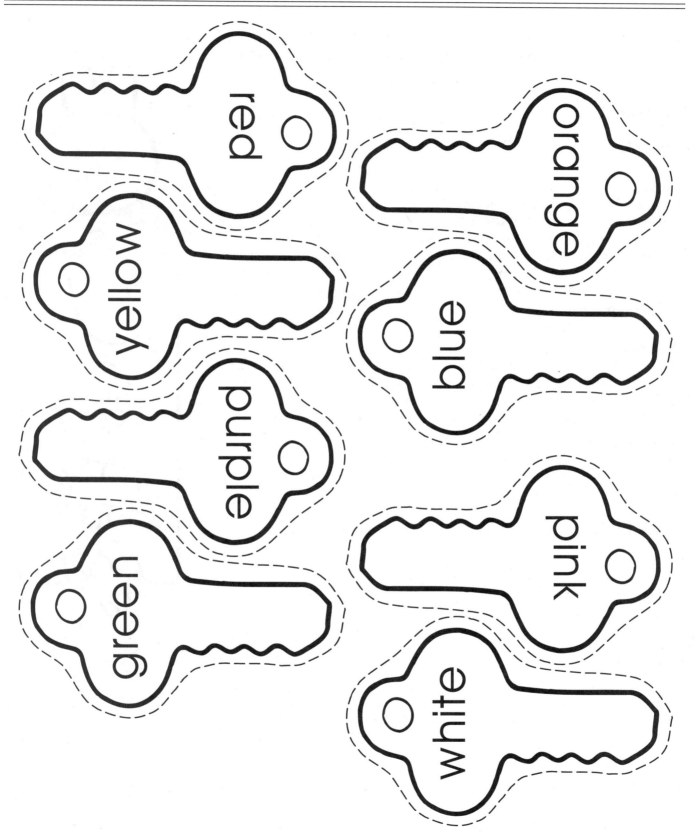

The Mitten
A Quick Trick with a Mitten

Children will adore the sequencing activity based on this famous Ukrainian folktale.

Materials:
Mitten
Small plastic animals

Directions:
1. Read the story to the children.
2. Place the mitten in the center of the circle.
3. As you re-read the story, have the children place the small plastic animals in the mitten. (If you don't have exact matches for the animals, you can change the words in the story to match. For instance, a zebra, a lion, and a koala bear might all find shelter in the mitten!)

Options:
• Use the patterns on the next page to make a mitten and animals. Duplicate the mitten twice and cut out. Create a pocket by stapling or taping three sides, leaving the top part open. Children can take turns sliding the animal patterns into the mitten. Number the animal patterns and have the children put them in based on numerical order.
• Make a mitten and set of patterns for each child to play with.
• Use the patterns on a bulletin board.

Book Link:
The Mitten by Jan Brett

Ten Apples Up on Top!
A Quick Trick with Apples

After doing this fun activity, children can have an apple snack!

Materials:
Apples
Basket

Directions:
1. Read the story of the three animals playing with apples. In the story, three different characters try to outdo each other by placing more and more apples on their heads.
2. As you read the story, have the children take turns taking an apple from the basket and placing it in a line. They can keep going all the way to ten.

Option:
Use the patterns on the next page to make apples, tigers, dogs, and lions. Give each child ten apples and one of the animal patterns. As you read the story, the children can place the apples on the tops of their patterns. At the end, the children can glue the patterns to heavy paper and color them in.

Book Link:
Ten Apples Up On Top! by Dr. Seuss, writing as Theo LeSieg

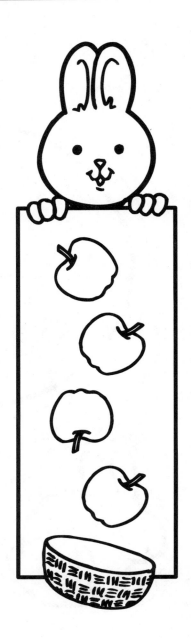

Ten Apples Up on Top

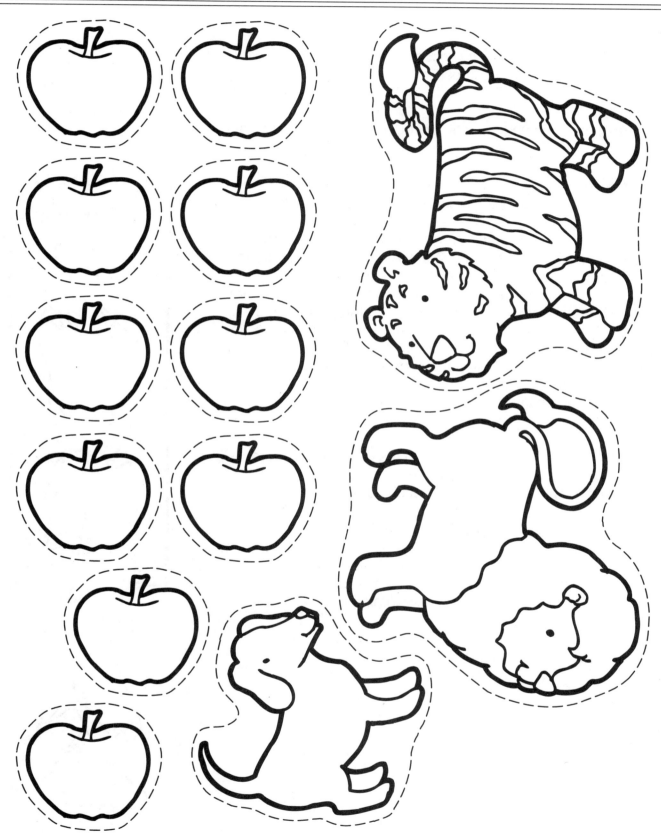

Blue Hat, Green Hat
A Quick Trick with Dress-Up Clothes

This fun book focuses on color recognition and the proper way to wear an assortment of clothes.

Materials:
Dress-up clothes, including hats, shirts, pants, coats, socks, and shoes

Directions:
1. Gather an assortment of dress-up clothes for the children to wear.
2. Read the story to the children then let children take turns acting out the parts in the story! Choose four children to dress up at a time. Three of the children should put on the right clothes in the right way, the fourth should make a mistake each time! (The teacher could also act out this fourth part.) If you don't have matches for the clothing in the story, read the book substituting the clothing that you do have. (The children should put the clothing on over their clothes–they don't have to be undressed like the animals in the book!)
3. Give all of the children an opportunity to dress up.

Options:
• Use the patterns on the next page to make a flannel board activity. Duplicate the patterns four times, color to match the items in the story, and cut out. Glue a piece of flannel to the back of each pattern. As you read the story, have the children place the different clothing patterns on a flannel board.
• Have the children draw pictures of themselves. Give each child a sheet of clothing patterns to cut out and glue onto their pictures. They can glue the clothing on in the correct places (a hat on the head) or they can glue the clothing on in a silly way.

Book Link:
Blue Hat, Green Hat by Sandra Boynton

Blue Hat, Green Hat

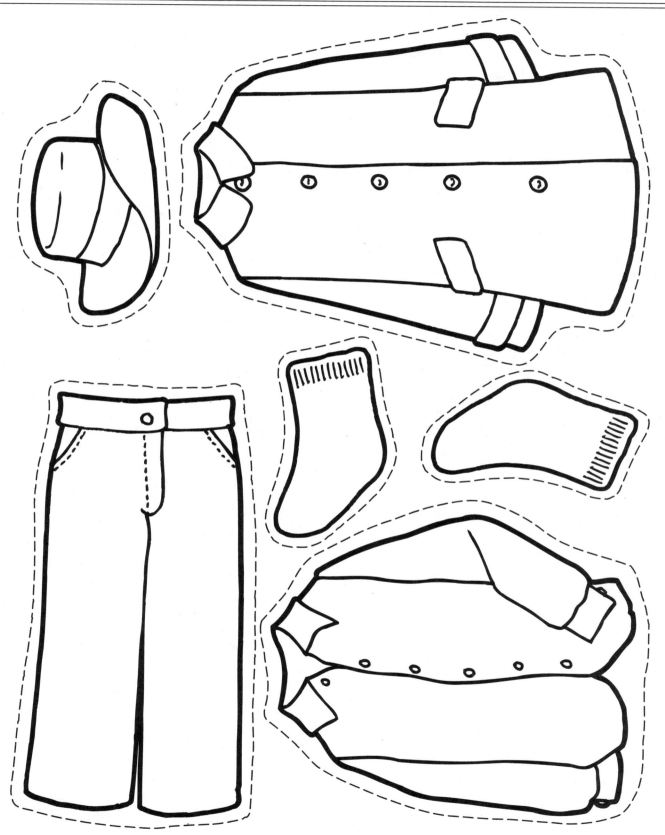

Mr. Brown Can Moo! Can You?
A Quick Trick with Sounds

Children will reinforce their knowledge of the noises different animals (and objects) make.

Materials:
Nothing

Directions:
1. Have the children sit in a circle as you read the story.
2. Give the children the chance to make the different noises featured in the story.
3. Once you've finished reading, have the children each suggest a different animal or object. Then let the class make the sound that the animal or object makes. For instance, the school bell, a car horn, a cat, a train, an airplane, a door slamming, and so on.

Option:
Duplicate the patterns on the next page for children to color and cut out. Give each child several sheets of paper, stapled at one side to make a book. Have the children glue the animal patterns to the pages and color as desired. Help the children write in the correct animal sound for each animal. The children can draw additional animals and sounds. Title each child's book, "_____'s Book of Wonderful Animal Sounds."

Book Link:
Mr. Brown Can Moo! Can You? Dr. Seuss's Book of Wonderful Noises

Sheep In a Jeep
A Quick Trick with Cotton Balls

Fluffy white cotton balls will help children create the perfect sheep to fit in their own Jeeps.

Materials:
Cotton balls
Glue
Crayons or markers
Construction paper

Directions:
1. Read the children the story *Sheep In a Jeep*.
2. Give each child a sheet of construction paper and a handful of cotton balls.
3. Have each child draw a Jeep and fill the Jeep with glued-on cotton ball "sheep." They can add features using crayons or markers.
4. As a class, count how many sheep are in each child's Jeep.

Options:
• Duplicate the patterns on the next page. Have the children cut out the Jeep and glue it to a sheet of construction paper. Then have the children cut out the sheep and glue them in the Jeep. They can color their pictures.
• For a counting activity, give each child a Jeep and five sheep. Have the children place one sheep in the Jeep at a time. Then work with the children to subtract the sheep.
• Duplicate five Jeeps and five sheep. Color the Jeeps and sheep in pairs—a red Jeep and red sheep, blue Jeep and blue sheep, and so on. Have the children match the correct sheep and Jeeps.

Book Link:
Sheep In a Jeep by Nancy Shaw

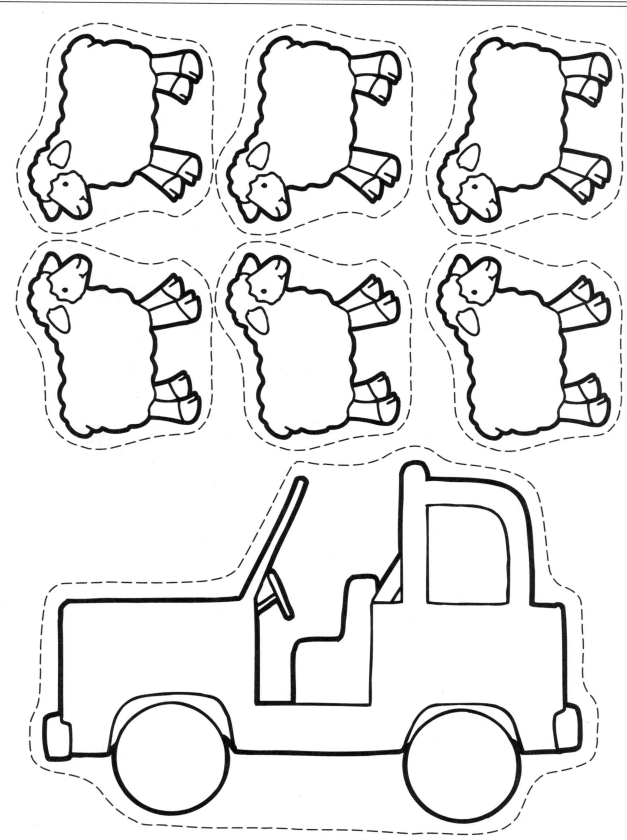

Mouse Paint
A Quick Trick with Food Coloring

Work with children on mixing an assortment of different colors after reading this delightful book.

Materials:
Food coloring
Water
Eyedroppers
Clear plastic cups
Newsprint

Directions:
1. Read *Mouse Paint*, emphasizing the theme of color-mixing.
2. Cover a workstation with newsprint. Then provide clear water in plastic cups and food coloring in eyedroppers.
3. Demonstrate how to mix colored water. Start with the primary colors: red, yellow, and blue. Then have the children use the eyedroppers to mix yellow and blue, red and yellow, and blue and red. Children can work in teams, as small groups, or on their own.

Options:
• Provide watercolor paints for the children to mix and paint with.
• Use the patterns to reinforce color-mixing skills. Duplicate a sheet for each child. Have the children color the paint containers correctly. Then have the children manipulate the patterns as you discuss color mixing. For instance, have them line up red and blue in front of purple. When you are finished, the children can glue all the patterns to a sheet of construction paper.

Book Link:
Mouse Paint by Ellen Stoll Walsh

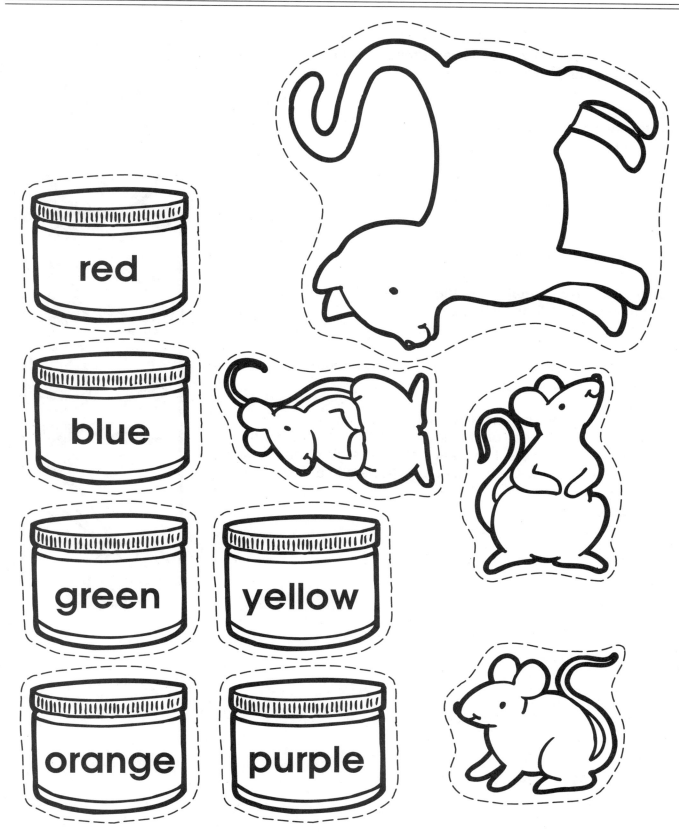

red

blue

green

yellow

orange

purple

Chrysanthemum
A Quick Trick with Construction Paper

Create a classroom flower or flower arrangement based on the names of the children in your class.

Materials:
Colored construction paper
Paper plate
Glue
Scissors
Crayons or markers

Directions:
1. Cut the colored construction paper into petal-shapes.
2. Read the children the story Chrysanthemum.
3. Give each child a petal. Have the children write their names on the petals. (Help those who need it!)
4. One at a time, have the children glue the petals around the paper plate center.
5. Post the completed name flower in your classroom.

Option:
Duplicate the flower patterns. Give each child one. Have the children write their names on the flowers and color the patterns using crayons or markers. Have each child glue his or her flower to a pipe cleaner stem. Gather the name flowers in a vase.

Book Link:
Chrysanthemum by Kevin Henkes

Chrysanthemum

A Color of His Own
A Quick Trick with Beanbags

This beanbag toss reinforces color words.

Materials:
Beanbags in assorted colors
Large sheet of poster board
Colored markers
Wiggly eyes and glue (optional)

Directions:
1. Create a grid on a large sheet of poster board. Make different squares of colors that match the colors of your beanbags.
2. If desired, glue wiggly eyes on your beanbags.
3. Read *A Color of His Own* to the children.
4. Have the children do a beanbag toss, trying to match the colored beanbag "chameleons" with the colored squares. The children should name the colors that the beanbags land on, even if the beanbags don't land on matching colors.

Option:
Use the patterns for a color-matching game. Duplicate two sets of chameleons onto heavy paper. Color them according to the color words. Have the children turn the patterns face down and play a concentration color-matching game.

Book Link:
A Color of His Own by Leo Lionni

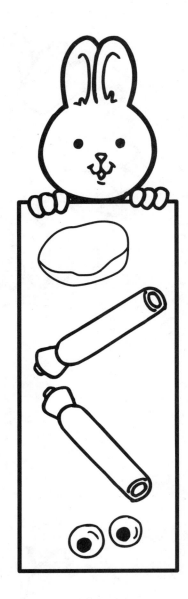

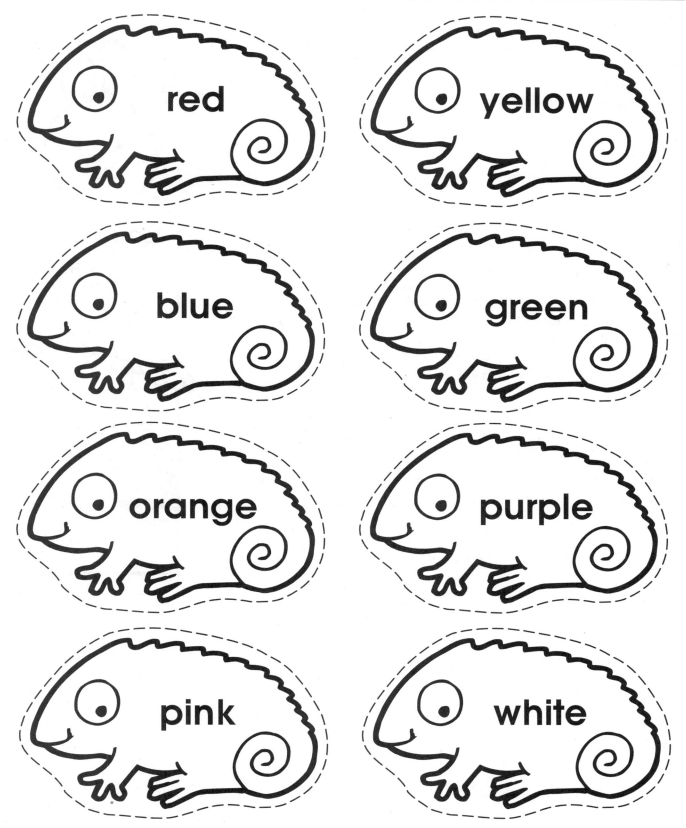

red

yellow

blue

green

orange

purple

pink

white

Harold and the Purple Crayon
A Quick Trick with Crayons

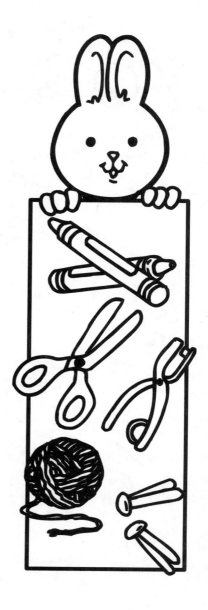

Children will have a chance to star in their own storybooks.

Materials:
White paper
Crayons
Scissors
Hole punch
Yarn or brads or a stapler

Directions:
1. Create mini-books for the children by cutting paper into squares and binding several sheets together with yarn, brads, or a stapler.
2. Read the children the story *Harold and the Purple Crayon*.
3. Let the children each choose one color crayon to work with.
4. Have the children draw pictures in each page of their books using only their chosen color.
5. Label the books with the children's names, for instance, "Devon and the Orange Crayon."

Options:
• Duplicate the patterns. Give each child one crayon to glue to the front of his or her book.
• Duplicate a sheet for each child. Have the children glue the crayons onto the crayon box and color each crayon using the correct color.

Book Link:
Harold and the Purple Crayon by Crockett Johnson

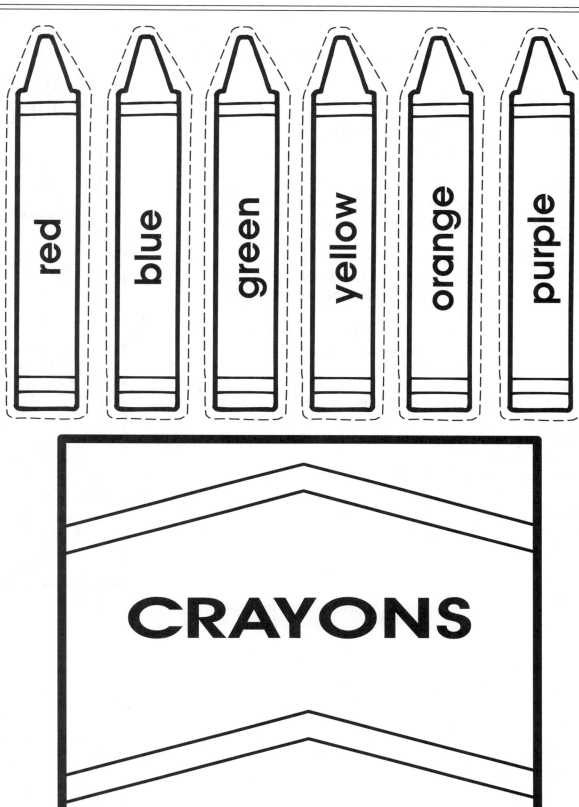

Blueberries for Sal
A Quick Trick with Plastic Pails

Turn your children into berry-hunters in the wilds of your classroom.

Materials:
Plastic pails (several for children to share)
Plastic counters (blue, if possible)

Directions:
1. Place blue counters around the room at child level. If plastic counters aren't available, cut circles from blue construction paper.
2. Read *Blueberries for Sal* to the children.
3. Have the children walk around the room looking for the "blueberries" (counters). When they find the counters, they should place them in the pails.
4. Gather the children together and work as a class to count the number of "blueberries" in each group's pail.

Options:
• Duplicate the patterns. Give each child one pail. Have the children cut out the pails and glue them onto a sheet of construction paper. Have them "fill" the pails with blueberries drawn on with blue crayons.
• Serve blueberries at snack time.

Book Link:
Blueberries for Sal by Robert McCloskey

I Went Walking
A Quick Trick with Construction Paper

A walk in the neighborhood, on the school grounds, or even in the classroom will provide inspiration for mini-books.

Materials:
Construction paper
Crayons
Scissors
Stapler or brads and a hole punch

Directions:
1. Read *I Went Walking* to the children.
2. Take the children on a walk–either outside the school or in the classroom. Challenge the children to pay attention to the different sights that they see on their walk. Give each child a chance to point out something that he or she sees.
3. Give each child a sheet of construction paper. Have the children draw pictures of items they saw on their walk.
4. Gather the pages together to make a "What We Saw" class book.

Option:
Duplicate the book patterns and make a book for each child. Have the children draw pictures of items they saw on their walks. Bind the books with staples, brads, or yarn.

Book Link:
I Went Walking by Sue Williams

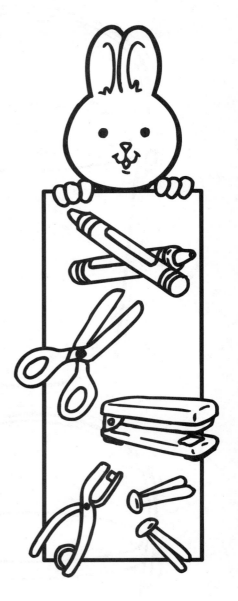

What I Saw

The Shape of Me
A Quick Trick with Shapes

Dr. Seuss's famous shape book will open the door for a shape-collecting activity.

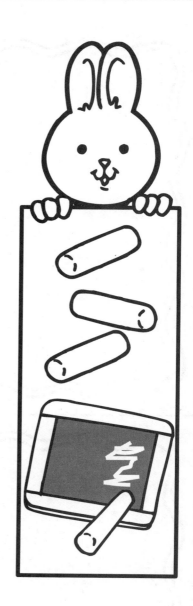

Materials:
Chalkboard
Chalk

Directions:
1. Read *The Shape of Me* to the children.
2. Challenge the children to spot different shapes in the classroom. Have the children find circles, squares, rectangles, triangles, and so on. For example, the globe or a rubber ball could be a circle, a book might be a rectangle, and a table might be square.
3. Create a chart on the chalkboard of all the different shapes found in the classroom: how many circles, squares, and so on.

Options:
• Duplicate a copy of the shape patterns for each child to color and cut out. The children can glue these shapes onto colored construction paper to make a variety of different designs.
• Trace around the children on large sheets of butcher paper so that each child will own a "shape of me."

Book Link:
The Shape of Me and Other Stuff: Dr. Seuss's Surprising Word Book

The Shape of Me

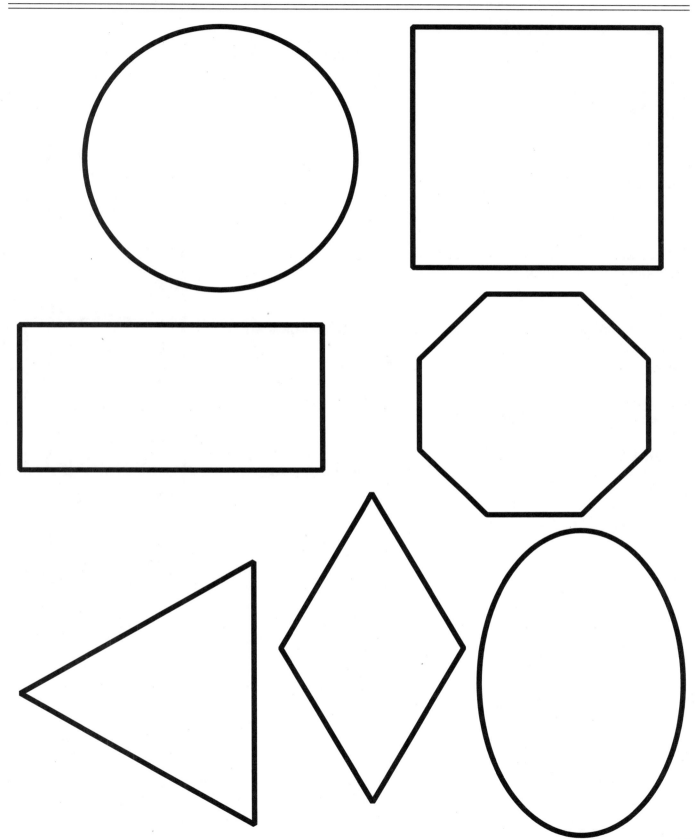

The Jolly Postman
A Quick Trick with Envelopes

Children adore "writing" letters and placing them in envelopes.

Materials:
Envelopes (one per child)
Paper
Crayons or markers

Directions:
1. Read *The Jolly Postman* to the children.
2. Give each child a sheet of paper. Have the children draw pictures or "write" letters on their papers.
3. Give each child an envelope. The children can place their letters in the envelopes.

Options:
• Help the children address their envelopes and exchange them with friends.
• Work as a class to write a letter to a favorite storybook character.
• Duplicate the envelope pattern. Children follow the directions to create their own envelopes.

Book Link:
The Jolly Postman: Or Other People's Letters by Janet & Allan Ahlberg

The Jolly Postman

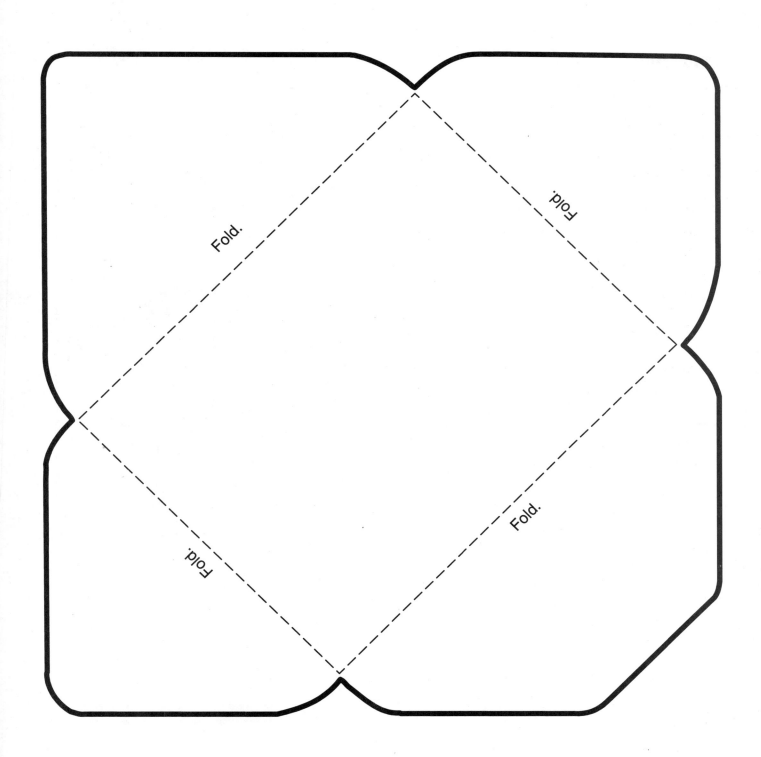

Pat the Bunny
A Quick Trick with Cotton Balls

Children will focus on creating fun, furry creations from cotton balls. Any touch-and-feel type of book will work with this activity.

Materials:
Cotton balls (colored, if desired)
Construction paper
Crayons or markers
Glue

Directions:
1. Read *Pat the Bunny* to the children.
2. Have the children draw bunnies on sheets of construction paper.
3. Provide cotton balls for the children to glue to their bunnies.
4. Post the 3-D bunnies in a tactile display at child-height.

Options:
• Duplicate a copy of the bunny pattern for each child. Children can glue cotton balls to the bunny.
• Provide assorted touch-and-feel materials for children to create other pictures: sandpaper, clear cellophane, aluminum foil, and so on.

Book Links:
• *Pat the Bunny* by Dorothy Kunhardt
• *Pat the Puppy* by Edith Kunhardt

Pat the Bunny

The Wheels on the Bus
A Quick Trick with Small Plastic Lids

Children create their own verses for this famous song.

Materials:
Small plastic lids
Construction paper
Crayons or markers
Glue

Directions:
1. Read *The Wheels on the Bus* to the children.
2. Give each child a sheet of construction paper.
3. Have the children draw buses on their papers. They can use the lids to trace the circle wheels on the buses. Or they can glue the lids onto the paper to create wheels.
4. Have the children illustrate one verse from the song–or create their own verse. For instance, they might draw the windshield wipers going back and forth or the windows going up and down. Or they might create a new verse by showing a dog barking in the back of the bus, or a bird chirping on top of the bus.

Options:
• Duplicate a copy of the bus pattern for each child. Children can color the buses and then illustrate one verse from the song.
• Play a recorded version of the song for the children to hear.

Book Links:
• *The Wheels on the Bus* by Raffi
• *The Wheels on the Bus* by Paul O. Zelinksy

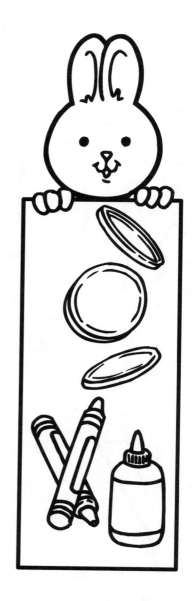

The Wheels on the Bus

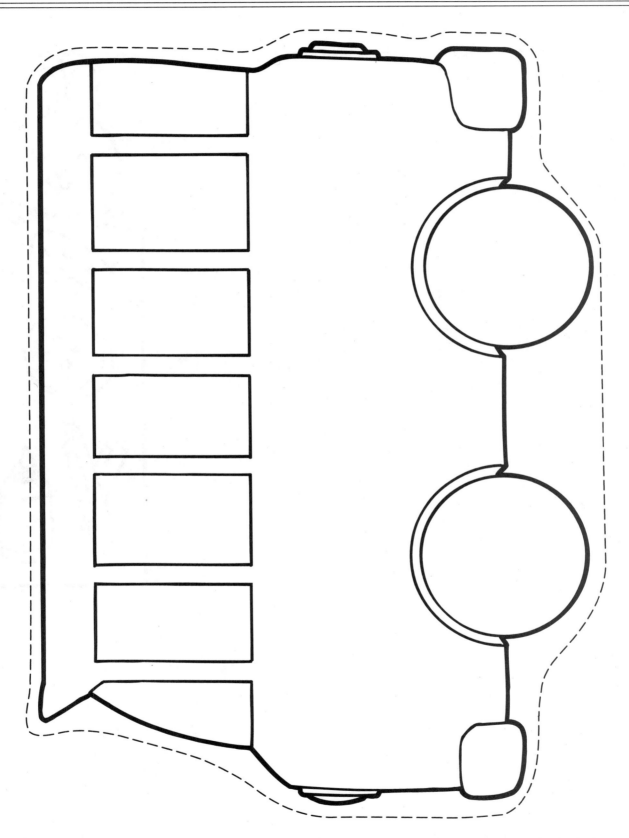

Miss Mary Mack
A Quick Trick with Buttons

Children become the stars of this whimsical rhyme.

Materials:
Buttons
Glue
Paper
Crayons or markers

Directions:
1. Read *Miss Mary Mack* to the children, or recite the rhyme.
2. Give each child a sheet of construction paper.
3. Have the children draw self-portraits.
4. Provide buttons for the children to glue to their self-portraits. (If your children are too young to work with buttons, cut out button-shapes from construction paper or felt.)
5. Read the story again, replacing each child's name for "Miss Mary Mack." For instance, you might sing, "Mr. Michael Stinson," or "Miss Kim Velez" in place of "Miss Mary Mack." (The names don't have to fit precisely.)

Options:
• Duplicate a copy of the elephant pattern for each child. Have the children draw themselves jumping the fence with the elephant.
• Duplicate the button patterns for the children to cut out and glue to their self-portraits.

Book Link:
Miss Mary Mack adapted by Mary Ann Hoberman

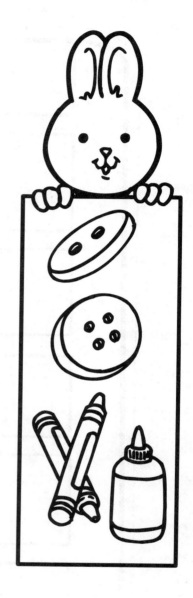

Miss Mary Mack

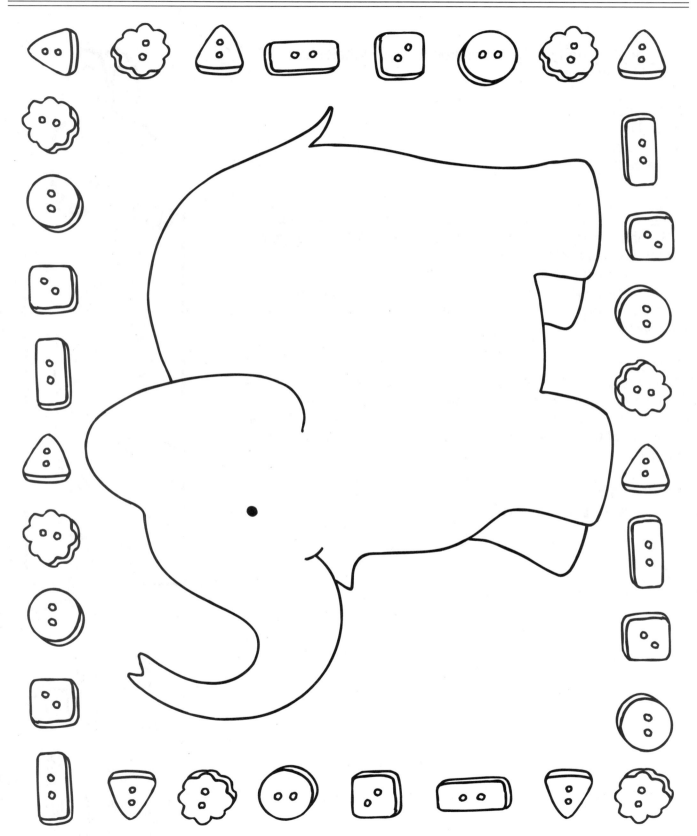

I'm a Little Teapot
A Quick Trick with Paper Cups

Time for a tea party for your children and all of their stuffed animal friends.

Materials:
Stuffed animals
Paper cups
Large quilt

Directions:
1. Ask each child to bring a stuffed animal or doll to school.
2. Spread a quilt on the floor and invite the children and their stuffed friends to sit in a circle.
3. Give each child a paper cup.
4. Read the children *I'm a Little Teapot* or teach them the song.
5. The children and their toy friends can enjoy pretend tea at their party.

Options:
• Serve juice and cookies or crackers at the tea party.
• Duplicate a copy of the teapot patterns for the children to color, cut out, and glue to construction paper. They can add additional drawings of themselves and their stuffed animal friends to the picture.

Book Link:
I'm a Little Teapot illustrated by Moira Kemp

I'm a Little Teapot

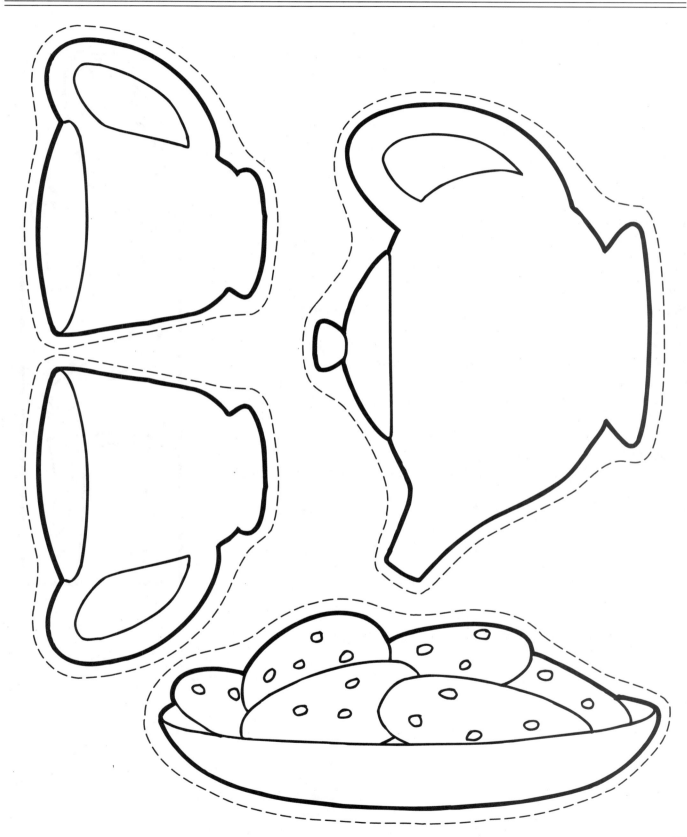

Make Way for Ducklings
A Quick Trick with Plastic Eggs

Children will be excited to watch these plastic eggs "hatch." This is a fun activity for the start of a school year.

Materials:
Plastic eggs (one per child)
Small pieces of paper
Marker
Brown paper bag

Directions:
1. Write each child's name on a piece of paper and place each paper slip in an egg.
2. Shred the edges of a paper bag to create a nest, and place the eggs in the nest.
3. Gather the children in a circle and place the nest in the center.
4. Read *Make Way for Ducklings* to the children. Then invite each child, one at a time, to pick an egg from the nest.
5. The children open the eggs and then give the eggs to the person whose name is on the paper inside. (Help children read the names, if necessary.)

Options:
• Duplicate the duck patterns. Write each child's name on a duck and place the ducks in the eggs.
• Create a *Make Way for Ducklings* bulletin board. Use the activity to discuss safety rules for crossing a street.

Note:
Plastic eggs are usually available around Easter time.

Book Link:
Make Way for Ducklings by Robert McCloskey, a Caldecott Award Book

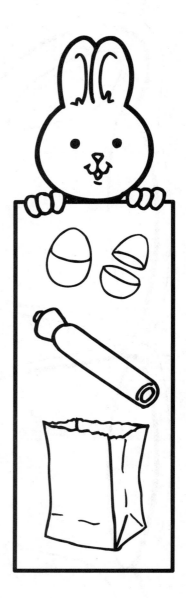

Make Way for Ducklings

Mr. Rabbit and the Lovely Present
A Quick Trick with Fruit

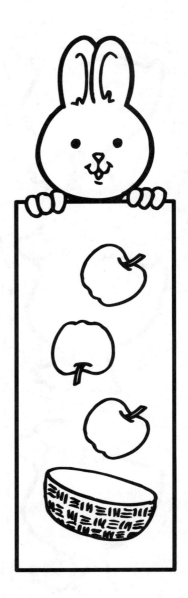

This is the perfect pre-snack activity. After filling the basket, serve a fruit salad for snack time.

Materials:
Assorted fruits (bananas, apples, oranges, and so on)
Basket

Directions:
1. Put the empty basket on the floor. Keep the fruit in your lap or in a bag.
2. Read *Mr. Rabbit and the Lovely Present* to the children.
3. Add a piece of fruit to the basket each time fruit is added in the story. If possible, match the fruits in the story. If not, use whatever is available.
4. Ask the children to think of other items that match the colors on each page of the story.

Option:
Duplicate the fruit patterns for each child. Have the children draw baskets on large sheets of paper. They can color, cut out, and glue the fruit patterns to their baskets.

Book Link:
Mr. Rabbit and the Lovely Present by Charlotte Zolotow

Where the Wild Things Are
A Quick Trick with Imaginations

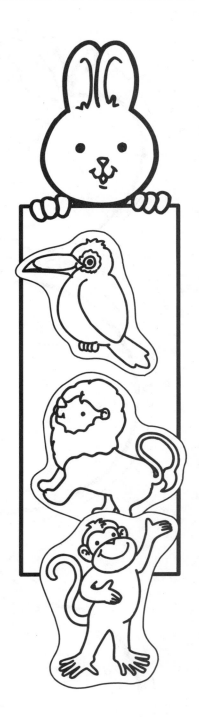

Get out any extra energy with a wild rumpus!

Materials:
Nothing

Directions:
1. Read *Where the Wild Things Are* to the children.
2. When you reach the part in the story where the wild things have a "rumpus," let the children march around the room, acting out the role of wild thing. You could choose one child to play Max and lead the others. If so, give each child a chance to be the leader.
3. Have the children sit down in a circle as you read the rest of the story.

Option:
Duplicate the jungle patterns for each child. Have the children draw pictures of their bedrooms. Give each child a sheet of jungle patterns to glue to their pictures, turning their bedrooms into jungles, just like Max's.

Book Link:
Where the Wild Things Are by Maurice Sendak

It Looked Like Spilt Milk
A Quick Trick with White Paint

Take children outside to look at clouds before doing this activity.

Materials:
Blue construction paper
White paint
Paintbrushes, eyedroppers, sponges

Directions:
1. Read *It Looked Like Spilt Milk* to the children.
2. Give each child a sheet of blue construction paper.
3. Provide an assortment of items for children to use to create clouds. They might sponge-print paint, use brushes, or gently squirt paint onto their papers with eyedroppers.
4. Once the pictures dry, post them all together on a "Cloudy Day" bulletin board. Have children try to see different shapes in the cloud pictures.

Option:
Duplicate a cloud pattern for each child. Write each child's name on a cloud. Use these to label the children's completed pictures.

Book Link:
It Looked Like Spilt Milk by Charles G. Shaw

If You Give a Moose a Muffin
A Quick Trick with Socks

Create a simple stage for puppet shows by turning a large cardboard box upside down and cutting a window in one side. Children climb inside the box and stage the show from inside.

Materials:
Socks (one per child)
Felt scraps
Yarn
Glue
Scissors

Directions:
1. Read *If You Give a Moose a Muffin* to the children.
2. Give each child a sock.
3. Children can cut features for their puppets from felt scraps. (Or cut out features–eyes, noses, tongues, and so on–ahead of time.)
4. Have children glue the felt features and yarn hair to their socks.
5. Children can work together to stage puppet shows for each other. They might act out books they've read or songs or nursery rhymes they know.

Options:
• Duplicate the patterns for children to cut out and glue to their sock puppets.
• Serve muffins at snack time.

Book Link:
If You Give a Moose a Muffin by Laura Joffe Numeroff

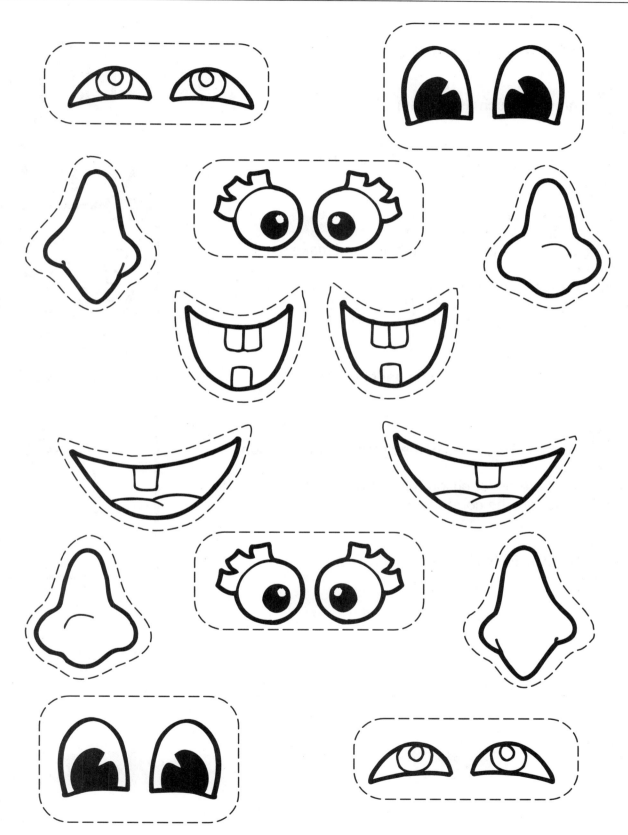

The Carrot Seed
A Quick Trick with Seeds

Introduce children to the wonders of growing plants.

Materials:
Seeds (fast-growing, such as parsley)
Soil
Water
Paper cups (or sections cut from egg containers)

Directions:
1. Read *The Carrot Seed* to the children.
2. Give each child a small paper cup.
3. Have the children fill their cups with soil and make small indents in the soil.
4. Provide seeds for children to plant, then cover with soil.
5. Help children water their plants. Then place the cups in a sunny spot. Water as needed.

Note:
Ahead of time, poke a hole in each paper cup for water drainage.

Options:
• Children can chart the stages of their plant's growth on long sheets of paper.
• Duplicate the patterns for children to color, cut out, and glue to construction paper in the correct order.

Book Link:
The Carrot Seed by Ruth Krauss

The Three Little Pigs
A Quick Trick with Straws

Share a variety of versions of this famous story with the children.

Materials:
Straws
Small empty milk cartons (three per child)
Twigs or craft sticks
Red construction paper
Black crayons
Glue
Scissors

Directions:
1. Read or tell a version of *The Three Little Pigs* to the children.
2. Have the children create houses for the three little pigs. They can glue straws to the first carton, twigs or craft sticks to the second, and red construction paper to the third. Children can draw squares onto the red paper to create bricks.
3. Set up a display area where children can create a town from their milk box houses.
4. Have children count the houses in their Pig Town.

Options:
• Use empty juice boxes in place of milk cartons.
• Duplicate the animal patterns for the children. Children can cut out and glue a pig to each house and the wolf to a craft stick for a puppet.

Book Links:
The Three Pigs by Paul Galdone
The True Story of The 3 Little Pigs by A. Wolf by Jon Scieszka
The Three Little Wolves and the Big Bad Pig by Eugene Trivizas

The Three Little Pigs

The Stupids Step Out
A Quick Trick with Crayons

Children create their own silly family portraits after listening to the story of the Stupids!

Materials:
Paper
Crayons or markers

Directions:
1. Read *The Stupids Step Out* to the children.
2. Have the children draw silly versions of their families. They might draw odd clothes or hats in their pictures. Or they might use silly color choices for eyes, hair, and so on.
3. Let the children dictate the silliest story that they can remember about their families. Write the story beneath the picture–or on the back.
4. Children can share their pictures and stories with the class.

Options:
• Ask the children to bring in photographs of their families. Children can create cards with the photograph glued to the front and the silly portrait on the inside.
• Duplicate a copy of the picture frame pattern for each child. Children can draw their silly family portraits in the frames.

Book Link:
The Stupids Step Out by Harry Allard

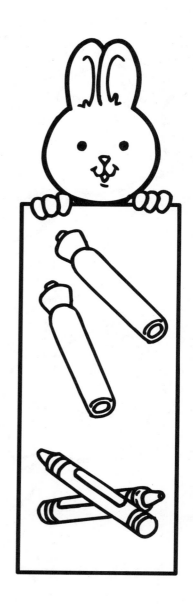

The Stupids Step Out

Curious George Gets a Medal
A Quick Trick with Aluminum Foil

Curious George was awarded a medal as the first space monkey. Children can make their own awards from foil-covered lids.

Materials:
Aluminum foil
Small plastic lids (one per child)
Hole punch
Yarn
Scissors

Directions:
1. Read *Curious George Gets a Medal* to the children.
2. Give each child a small plastic lid.
3. Show the children how to cover the lids with aluminum foil.
4. Punch a hole in each lid and thread through with a long piece of yarn. Tie the ends to create a necklace.

Options:
• Write the children's names on labels and place these on the lids.
• Have children decorate their lids by gluing on glitter or sequins.
• Use the medal patterns for children to create their own awards.

Book Links:
Curious George Gets a Medal by H.A. Rey
To Hilda for Helping by Margot Zemach

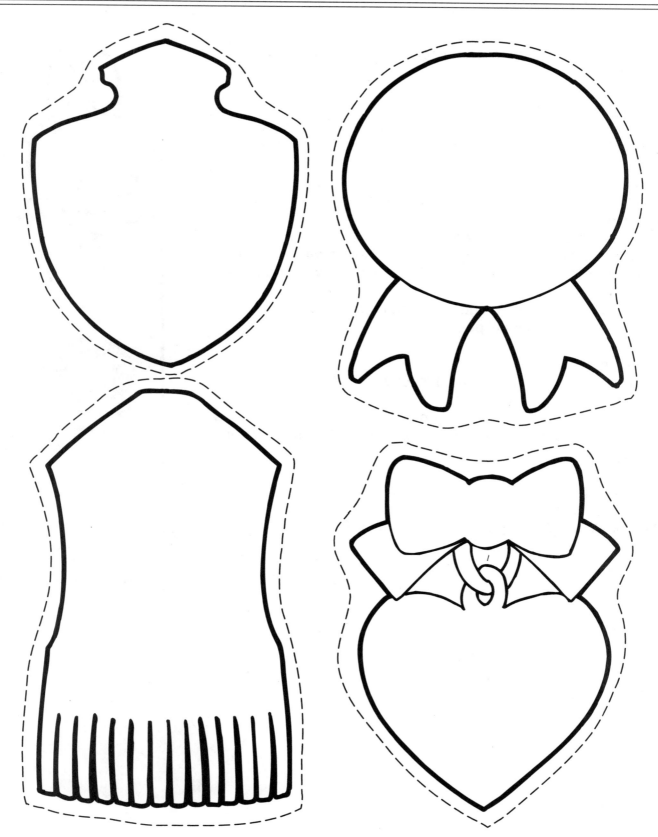

Strega Nona
A Quick Trick with White Yarn

Children will have fun creating magic spaghetti pots filled with yarn pasta.

Materials:
White yarn
Small paper cups (one per child)
Glue
Foil (optional)

Directions:
1. Read *Strega Nona* to the children.
2. Give each child a small paper cup to fill with strands of white yarn. Children can glue pieces of the yarn overflowing from the cups.
3. Children can cover the outside of the cup with foil to make it look more like a spaghetti pot.

Options:
• Serve spaghetti at snack time. Flavor with butter or parmesan cheese.
• Duplicate the patterns for children to cut out and glue to sheets of paper. They can draw pictures around the patterns to recreate the story.

Book Links:
• *Strega Nona* by Tomie de Paola
• *Strega Nona's Magic Lessons* by Tomie de Paola

Mushroom in the Rain
A Quick Trick with Egg Cartons

Create a whole field of colorful mushrooms in your classroom.

Materials:
Egg cartons
Scissors
Corks
Tempera paint
Paintbrushes
Glue
Clay

Directions:
1. Cut the egg cartons into individual sections.
2. Read *Mushroom in the Rain* to the children.
3. Give each child at least one egg carton section.
4. Have the children paint the egg carton sections, then let the sections dry.
5. Children then glue a cork base into each egg carton mushroom.
6. Stand the mushrooms on bookshelves, window ledges, and other places in the room by placing a small piece of clay on each cork bottom for a base.

Option:
Duplicate two sets of the mushroom patterns. Color the sets to match, cut out, laminate, and cut out again. Children can play concentration with the patterns.

Book Link:
Mushroom in the Rain by Mirra Ginsburg

Mushroom in the Rain

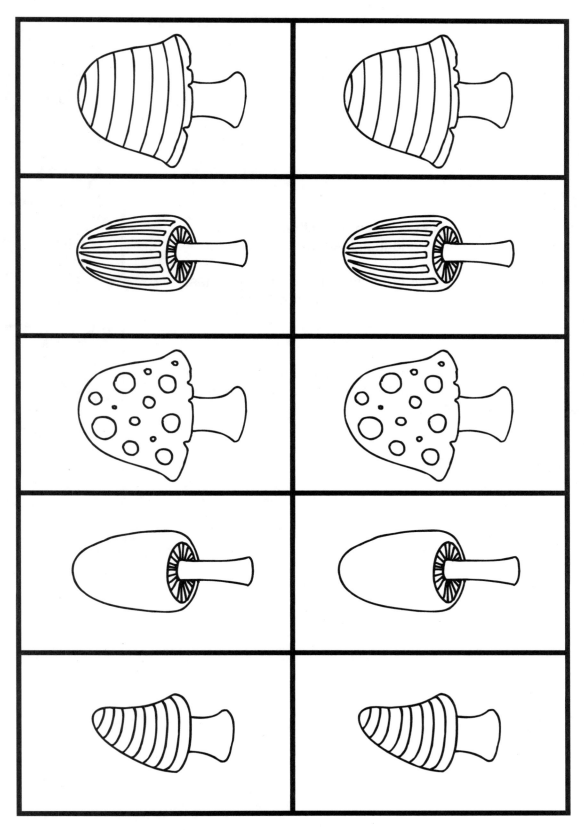

Madeline
A Quick Trick with Craft Sticks

Children will create two straight lines from craft stick characters.

Materials:
Craft sticks
Wiggly eyes
Glue
Markers

Directions:
1. Read *Madeline* to the children.
2. Give the children craft sticks to decorate with markers. Children can draw on clothes and facial features and glue on wiggly eyes.
3. Have the children place their craft sticks in two straight lines, just like the lines created by *Madeline* and the other children in the story.

Option:
Duplicate the weather patterns for each child. Have the children help create a weather-themed bulletin board. (Madeline and her peers stood in two straight lines in rain or shine!)

Book Link:
Madeline by Ludwig Bemelmans

Quick Tricks for Story Time ©2002 Monday Morning Books, Inc.

The Rainbow Fish
A Quick Trick with Aluminum Foil

These colorful fish glint in the light.

Materials:
Aluminum foil
Paper
Glue
Crayons or markers
Scissors
Hole punch
Yarn

Directions:
1. Read *The Rainbow Fish* to the children.
2. Give each child a sheet of paper. Have the children draw fish on their papers and cut them out. They should add colored scales using crayons or markers.
3. Children can tear small pieces of aluminum foil to glue to their fish.
4. Have the children decorate both sides of their fish.
5. Punch a hole in each fish and thread through with a piece of yarn. Hang the school of fish in the classroom.

Option:
Duplicate the fish patterns for the children to decorate with crayons, markers, and foil.

Book Link:
The Rainbow Fish by Marcus Pfister

Quick Tricks for Story Time ©2002 Monday Morning Books, Inc.

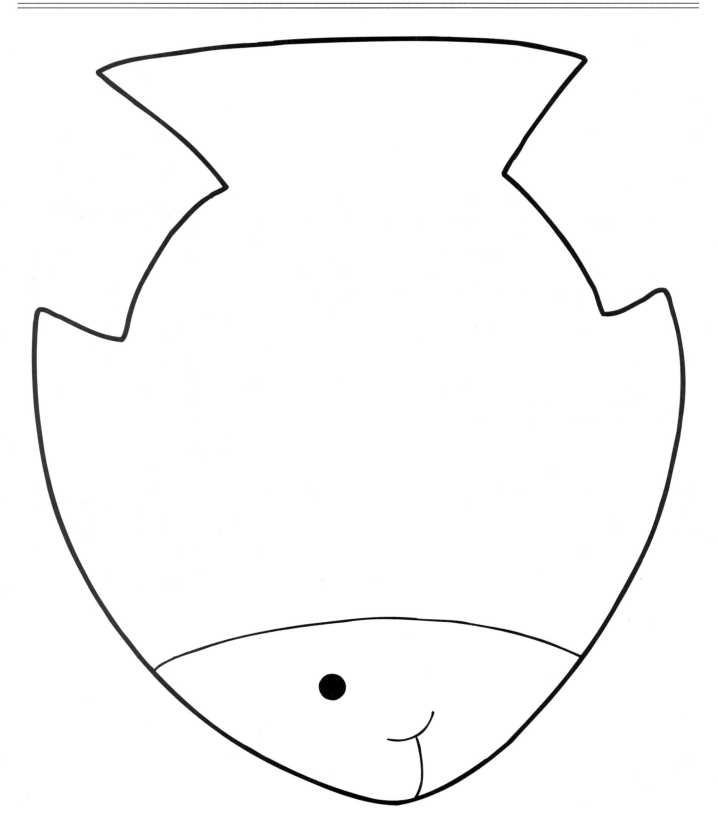

Caps for Sale
A Quick Trick with Circle Stickers

This is a fun lead-in to a counting activity.

Materials:
Circle stickers
Paper
Crayons or markers

Directions:
1. Read *Caps for Sale* to the children.
2. Give each child a sheet of paper. Explain that the children will be drawing pictures of themselves as the salesman in the story. Have the children draw self-portraits on their papers.
3. Provide circle stickers for children to use in place of the hats. They should stick one on top of the other to create tall towers of hats.
4. As a class, count the hats in the pictures.

Options:
• Duplicate the monkey and hat patterns for children to color, cut out, and glue to their pictures.
• Children could glue on circles of fabric in place of the circle stickers.

Book Link:
Caps for Sale: A Tale of a Peddler, Some Monkeys and Their Monkey Business by Esphyr Slobodkina

Caps for Sale

Little Red Riding Hood
A Quick Trick with Margarine Tubs

Read the children a few different versions of this often retold story.

Materials:
Margarine tubs (or other small containers with lids)
Construction paper
Scissors
Crayons or markers

Directions:
1. Read or tell the tale of *Little Red Riding Hood*.
2. Give each child a margarine tub. Explain that these are their baskets of goodies.
3. Have children create cookies and other goodies from construction paper and crayons or markers. They can store their goodies in their margarine tub baskets.
4. Children can act out the story, using the baskets they've created.

Options:
• Use the patterns on the next page to make puppets for use with the telling of this story. Duplicate the patterns onto heavy paper. Cut out the patterns, and add craft stick handles.
• Serve goodies (such as cookies) from a basket at snack time.

Book Links:
Little Red Riding Hood illustrated by Trina Schart Hyman
Petite Rouge: A Cajun Red Riding Hood by Mike Artell

Little Red Riding Hood

Cloudy with a Chance of Meatballs
A Quick Trick with Cotton Balls

This fanciful story is the perfect lead-in for a discussion of the changing weather.

Materials:
Cotton balls
Paper
Glue
Crayons or markers.

Directions:
1. Read *Cloudy with a Chance of Meatballs* to the children.
2. Give each child a sheet of paper. Explain that the children will be creating their own unique weather/food pictures.
3. Have children glue cotton ball clouds to their papers and then add any types of foods they want using crayons or markers.
4. Post the completed pictures on a Wacky Weather bulletin board.

Option:
Duplicate the food patterns for children to color, cut out, and incorporate into their pictures.

Book Links:
• *Cloudy with a Chance of Meatballs* by Judi Barrett
• *Pickles to Pittsburgh: The Sequel to Cloudy with a Chance of Meatballs* by Judi Barrett

The Lady with the Alligator Purse
A Quick Trick with Green Construction Paper

Children adore this whimsical chant!

Materials:
Green construction paper
Scissors
Stapler
Hole punch
Green yarn
Crayons or Markers

Directions:
1. Read *The Lady with the Alligator Purse* to the children.
2. Give each child a sheet of green paper to fold in half. Have each child draw an alligator's head on the paper, starting with the neck on the fold and the mouth toward the open end.
3. Help children cut out the pictures, keeping the fold intact.
4. Staple up the sides of each purse, leaving the top open.
5. Help children punch two holes in the tops of the purses and thread through with green yarn. Tie for a handle.

Options:
• This story is available as a book on tape.
• Children can draw white teeth and other features onto their purses.
• Duplicate two copies of the alligator pattern for each child. Children color and cut out the patterns. Help children tape or staple three sides closed. Punch holes and add yarn handles.

Book Link:
The Lady with the Alligator Purse by Nadine Bernard Westcott

The Lady with the Alligator Purse

Bugs in a Box
A Quick Trick with Colored Cotton Balls

Sort these unusual "bugs" by colors, too.

Materials:
Colored cotton balls
Box

Directions:
1. Gather the children in a circle and read *How Many Bugs in a Box?*
2. Place a box in the center of the circle.
3. Give each child a colored cotton ball.
4. Have the children place their cotton balls in the box, counting aloud as they add the "bugs."

Options:
• Children can glue on felt feet and add features with markers. Or glue on wiggly eyes.
• Duplicate the patterns for children to color and cut out. Use these bugs in place of the cotton balls.

Book Links:
• *How Many Bugs in a Box?* by David A Carter
• *Alphabugs* by David A. Carter
• *Bed Bugs* by David A. Carter
• *Giggle Bugs* by David A. Carter
• *Feely Bugs* by David A. Carter

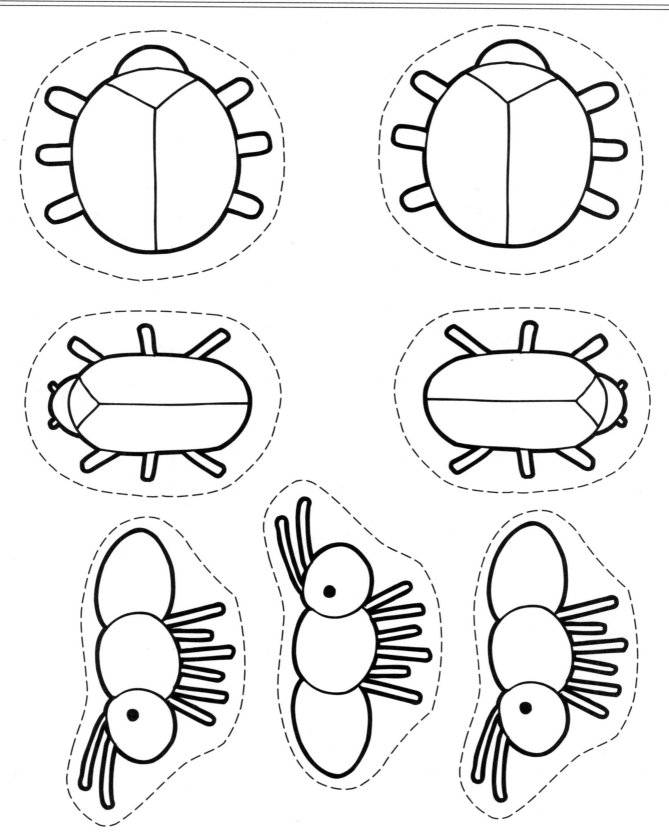

One Fine Day
A Quick Trick with Blue Beads

A fox trades a variety of different goods and services in an attempt to win back his tail.

Materials:
Blue beads
Yarn
Scissors

Directions:
1. Gather the children in a circle and read *One Fine Day*.
2. Give each child a blue bead and a length of yarn.
3. Children can thread the bead onto the yarn. Then help them tie the ends to make necklaces.

Options:
• Children can create their own blue beads from clay.
• Duplicate the bead patterns for children to cut out and color. Help children punch a hole in each pattern and then thread through with yarn or string. Children can wear the paper bead necklaces.

Book Link:
One Fine Day by Nonny Hogrogian

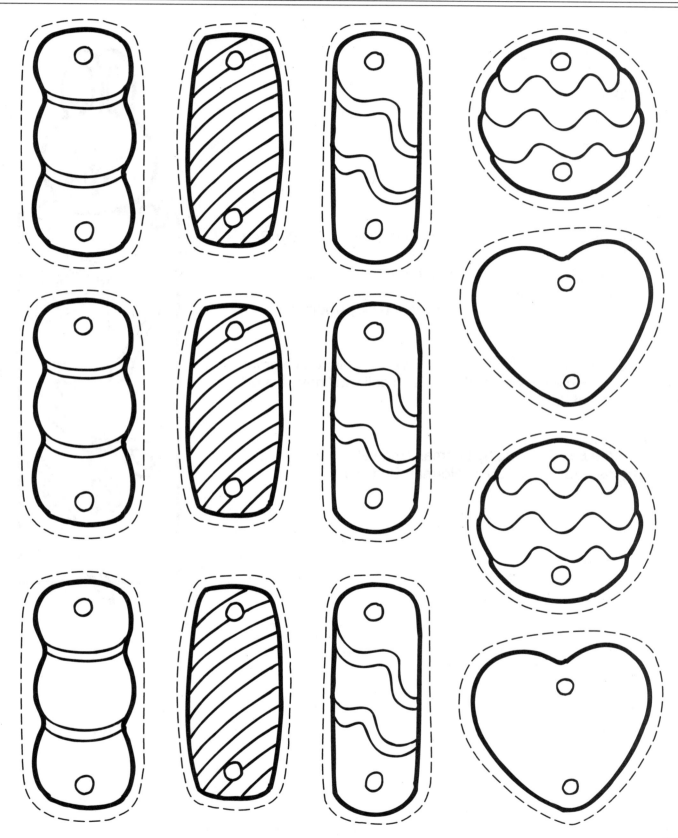

Clifford, the Big Red Dog
A Quick Trick with Red Paint

Make the biggest dog you can!

Materials:
Red paint
Paintbrushes
Butcher paper
Scissors
Pencil

Directions:
1. Gather the children in a circle and read *Clifford, the Big Red Dog.*
2. Trace a simple outline of a dog onto the butcher paper.
3. Children work together to paint the entire dog red.
4. Cut out the dog and post on a wall in the classroom.

Options:
Duplicate the pattern for each child. Have the children color the dogs red using crayons or markers. Each child will have his or her own big red dog.

Book Links:
• *Clifford, the Big Red Dog* by Norman Bridwell
• *Clifford the Firehouse Dog* by Norman Bridwell

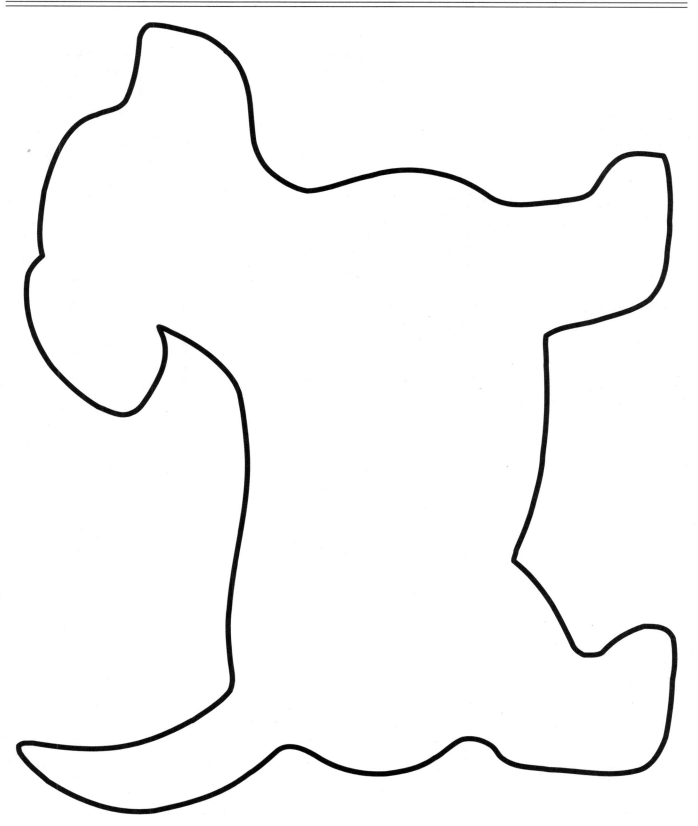

Tikki Tikki Tembo
A Quick Trick with Children's Names

Create an unusual name to rival *Tikki Tikki Tembo* from the names of the children in your class.

Materials:
Colored chalk
Chalk board

Directions:
1. Gather the children in a circle and read *Tikki Tikki Tembo*.
2. Work together as a class to create a long name from the children's names. Either write the children's names on the chalkboard, or let them write their names themselves on the board. Link the names with hyphens, for example, "Dana-Arlo-Madeline-Mary-Francis-Joshua..." until you have written all of the children's names on the board.
3. As a class, read the outlandishly long name!

Option:
Write the children's names on pieces of paper and post the names in a row around the room.

Book Link:
Tikki Tikki Tembo by Arlene Mosel

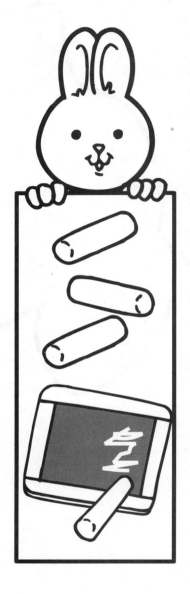